The Joy of Parenthood

EDITED BY SARAH ARAK

Cover design by Richard Garnas
Interior design and production by Patty Holden

ISBN: 1-59637-052-1

Printed and bound in China

Introduction

PARENTHOOD HAS BEEN DESCRIBED AS LIFE'S GREATEST
adventure. Like any great adventure, parenthood is full of unknowns. For new
parents, success often depends on the ability to improvise, notwithstanding the
fact that we have had our whole lives to observe our own mothers and fathers.
Alas, when it is our turn to take the stage we realize there are no dress rehearsals,
and no scripts to follow. We must rely on love and instinct to give, literally, the
performance of a lifetime.

Becoming a parent for the first time is an unprecedented emotional
experience, one that involves dramatic highs and lows as parents tumble through
alternating feelings of wonder, delight, paralyzing fear, and ecstatic joy. These
feelings are natural, and are part of the dynamic, evolving experience we
call parenthood.

For all parents, whether they're first-timers or veterans expecting their
fifth, the journey of parenthood is an unforgettable and joyous experience.

I UNDERSTOOD IMMEDIATELY

WHEN I HELD A BABY IN MY ARMS

WHY SOME PEOPLE HAVE THE NEED

TO KEEP HAVING THEM.

—Spalding Gray

MOTHER'S LOVE IS PEACE.

IT NEED NOT BE ACQUIRED,

IT NEED NOT BE DESERVED.

—Erich Fromm

IF PREGNANCY WERE A BOOK,

THEY WOULD CUT THE LAST

TWO CHAPTERS.

— Nora Ephron

WHEN MY KIDS BECOME WILD AND UNRULY,

I USE A NICE, SAFE PLAYPEN.

WHEN THEY'RE FINISHED, I CLIMB OUT.

—Erma Bombeck

YOU DON'T REALLY UNDERSTAND HUMAN NATURE

UNLESS YOU KNOW WHY A CHILD ON A MERRY-GO-ROUND

WILL WAVE AT HER PARENTS EVERY TIME AROUND —

AND WHY HER PARENTS WILL ALWAYS WAVE BACK.

— William D. Tammeus

MAKING THE DECISION TO HAVE

A CHILD—IT'S MOMENTOUS. IT IS TO

DECIDE FOREVER TO HAVE YOUR HEART GO

WALKING AROUND OUTSIDE YOUR BODY.

— Elizabeth Stone

THE GUYS WHO FEAR BECOMING FATHERS

DON'T UNDERSTAND THAT FATHERING

IS NOT SOMETHING PERFECT MEN DO, BUT

SOMETHING THAT PERFECTS THE MAN.

— Frank Pittman

Babies are infinitely more trouble

than you thought — and

infinitely more wonderful.

— Charles Osgood

B Y FAR THE MOST COMMON CRAVING OF

PREGNANT WOMEN IS NOT TO BE PREGNANT.

— Phyllis Diller

A BABY IS A BLANK CHECK MADE

PAYABLE TO THE HUMAN RACE.

—Barbara Christine Seifert

ANYONE WHO USES THE PHRASE

'EASY AS TAKING CANDY FROM A BABY'

HAS NEVER TRIED TAKING

CANDY FROM A BABY.

— Author Unknown

PREGNANT WOMEN...HAVE AN AURA OF MAGIC.

THEY COMPEL ATTENTION, CONSTANTLY

REMINDING YOU THAT THEY CARRY THE FUTURE

INSIDE—ITS CONTOURS ALREADY DRAWN,

BUT VEILED, PRIVATE, AN INNER SECRET.

—Ruth Morgan

HAVING A TODDLER IS LIKE

HAVING A BOWLING ALLEY

INSTALLED IN YOUR HEAD.

— Martin Mull

WHILE WE TRY TO TEACH OUR CHILDREN

ALL ABOUT LIFE, OUR CHILDREN TEACH US

WHAT LIFE IS ALL ABOUT.

—Author Unknown

WHAT GOOD MOTHERS AND FATHERS

INSTINCTIVELY FEEL LIKE DOING FOR THEIR

BABIES IS USUALLY BEST AFTER ALL.

—Benjamin Spock

THERE IS ONE ORDER OF BEAUTY WHICH

SEEMS MADE TO TURN HEADS. IT IS A BEAUTY

LIKE THAT OF KITTENS, OR VERY SMALL DOWNY DUCKS

MAKING GENTLE RIPPLING NOISES WITH THEIR

SOFT BILLS, OR BABIES JUST BEGINNING TO TODDLE.

— T.S. Eliot

Babies are such a nice way

to start people!

—Don Herrold

I DON'T KNOW WHY THEY SAY

'YOU HAVE A BABY.'

THE BABY HAS YOU!

— Gallagher

Even when freshly washed and

relieved of all obvious confections,

children tend to be sticky.

— Fran Lebowitz

THERE ARE TWO THINGS IN LIFE

FOR WHICH PARENTS ARE NEVER

TRULY PREPARED: TWINS.

—Josh Billings

UNTIL YOU HAVE A SON OF YOUR OWN...

YOU WILL NEVER KNOW THE JOY, THE LOVE

BEYOND FEELING THAT RESONATES IN THE HEART

OF A FATHER AS HE LOOKS UPON HIS SON.

—Kent Nerburn

IF EVOLUTION REALLY WORKS,

HOW COME MOTHERS ONLY

HAVE TWO HANDS?

— Milton Berle

Everybody knows how to raise children,

except the people who have them.

—P. J. O'Rourke

WHEN A CHILD IS BORN, A FATHER IS BORN.

A MOTHER IS BORN, TOO, OF COURSE, BUT AT

LEAST FOR HER IT'S A GRADUAL PROCESS. BUT FOR

EVEN THE BEST-PREPARED FATHER, IT HAPPENS

ALL AT ONCE—JUST AS IT DOES FOR THE CHILD.

— Frederick Buechner

RAISING KIDS IS PART JOY AND

PART GUERILLA WARFARE.

— Ed Asner

A BABY'S A FULL TIME JOB FOR THREE ADULTS.

NOBODY TELLS YOU THAT WHEN YOU'RE PREGNANT,

OR YOU'D PROBABLY JUMP OFF A BRIDGE. NOBODY

TELLS YOU HOW ALL-CONSUMING IT IS TO BE

A MOTHER—HOW READING GOES OUT THE

WINDOW, AND THINKING, TOO.

—Erica Jong

PEOPLE WHO SAY THEY SLEEP LIKE

BABIES USUALLY DON'T HAVE THEM.

—Leo J. Burke

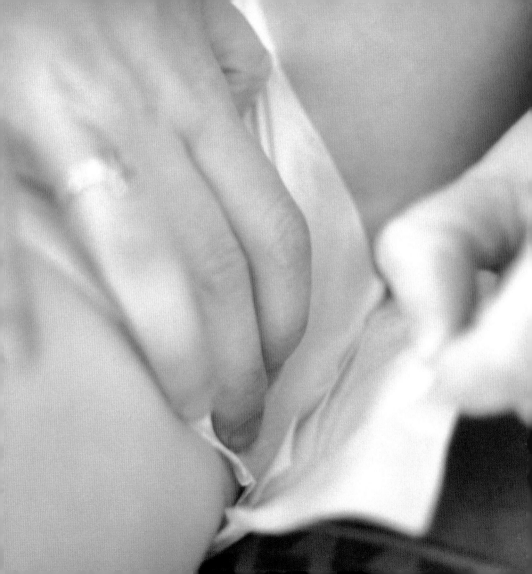

'DIAPER' SPELLED BACKWARD IS 'REPAID.'

THINK ABOUT IT.

— Marshall McLuhan

A FATHER IS SOMEONE WHO CARRIES

PICTURES WHERE HIS MONEY USED TO BE.

— Author Unknown

CHILD REARING MYTH #1:

LABOR ENDS WHEN THE BABY IS BORN.

—Author Unknown

IT SOMETIMES HAPPENS, EVEN IN THE BEST

OF FAMILIES, THAT A BABY IS BORN. THIS IS NOT

NECESSARILY CAUSE FOR ALARM. THE IMPORTANT

THING IS TO KEEP YOUR WITS ABOUT YOU

AND BORROW SOME MONEY.

— Eleanor Smith

I'VE GOT SEVEN KIDS. THE THREE WORDS

YOU HEAR MOST AROUND MY HOUSE ARE 'HELLO,'

'GOODBYE,' AND 'I'M PREGNANT.'

—Dean Martin

A BABY MAKES LOVE STRONGER,

DAYS SHORTER, NIGHTS LONGER, BANKROLLS SMALLER,

HOMES HAPPIER, CLOTHES SHABBIER, THE PAST FORGOTTEN,

AND THE FUTURE WORTH LIVING FOR.

— Author Unknown

A BABY IS GOD'S OPINION THAT

THE WORLD SHOULD GO ON.

—Carl Sandburg

A CHILD IS LIKE THE BEGINNING

OF ALL THINGS—WONDER, HOPE,

A DREAM OF POSSIBILITIES.

—Eda J. Le Shan

WE FIND DELIGHT IN THE BEAUTY AND

HAPPINESS OF CHILDREN THAT MAKES THE

HEART TOO BIG FOR THE BODY.

— Ralph Waldo Emerson

A BABY IS AN INESTIMABLE BOTHER

AND A BLESSING.

— Mark Twain

CERTAIN IS IT THAT THERE IS NO KIND OF

AFFECTION SO PURELY ANGELIC AS OF A FATHER

TO A DAUGHTER. IN LOVE TO OUR WIVES

THERE IS DESIRE; TO OUR SONS, AMBITION;

BUT TO OUR DAUGHTERS THERE IS SOMETHING

WHICH THERE ARE NO WORDS TO EXPRESS.

—Joseph Addison

PARENTS ARE OFTEN SO BUSY WITH THE

PHYSICAL REARING OF CHILDREN THAT THEY MISS

THE GLORY OF PARENTHOOD, JUST AS THE GRANDEUR

OF THE TREES IS LOST WHEN RAKING LEAVES.

— Marcelene Cox

THERE ARE TWO LASTING BEQUESTS

WE CAN GIVE OUR CHILDREN:

ONE IS ROOTS, THE OTHER IS WINGS.

—Hodding Carter

You CAN LEARN MANY THINGS FROM HAVING CHILDREN.

HOW MUCH PATIENCE YOU HAVE, FOR INSTANCE.

— Franklin P. Jones

OF ALL THE RIGHTS OF WOMEN,

THE GREATEST IS TO BE A MOTHER.

— Lin Yutang

PHOTO CREDITS